Nature's Children

OPOSSUM

Laima Dingwall

GROLIER
EDUCATIONAL

FACTS IN BRIEF

Classification of the Opossum

Class: *Mammalia* (mammals)
Order: *Marsupialia* (marsupials)
Family: *Didelphidae* (New World opposums)
Genus: *Didelphis*
Species: *Didelphis virginiana*

World distribution.   Exclusive to North and South America. Other marsupials are found in South America and Australia.

Habitat.   Woods, pastures and parks: areas where water is available are preferred.

Distinctive physical characteristics.   Fur-lined abdominal pouch on females; large thin black naked ears; long thin tail; large pink naked nose tip; white or black-tipped fur.

Habits.   Most active at night; can both climb trees and swim; lives in the abandoned burrows of other animals; will sometimes play dead if captured by a predator; younger ones can hang upside down from tree branches by their tails.

Published originally as
"Getting to Know . . . Nature's Children."

This series is approved and recommended by the Federation of Ontario Naturalists.

This library reinforced edition is available exclusively from:

GROLIER
EDUCATIONAL

Sherman Turnpike, Danbury, Connecticut 06816

Contents

If you have ever seen an opossum, you have seen one of the most unusual animals in North America. What is so remarkable about the opossum, or possum as some people call it?

Well, to begin with, the opossum is the only animal in North America that hangs upside down by its tail. More than that, it has "hands" on its back legs, "feet" on its front legs, and it carries its babies in a pouch on its stomach. Read on to find out more about this odd, shy little creature which much prefers to be left alone.

Long white hairs cover the black-tipped fur below, giving the opossum a silvery look.

Where's Mom?

Opossum babies are very attached to their mother. They spend their first six weeks of life in a warm furry pouch on her stomach. And even after they leave the pouch for good, they like to be near their mother. Sometimes they even hitch a ride on her back when they get tired.

But these three youngsters are old enough to be on their own. What is in store for them? Read on to find out.

Relatives Near and Far

If you could hop aboard a time machine and travel back 200 million years to the age of the dinosaurs, you would probably see the tiny opossum scurrying between the legs of the mighty Brontosaurus. There are no dinosaurs around today, but the opossum is still here.

The opossum belongs to a very ancient group of animals called the marsupials. Besides being old-timers, marsupials have something else in common. The female carries her babies in a fur-lined pouch on her belly.

The common, or Virginia Opossum, is the only marsupial that lives in North America. Scientists believe it traveled up from South America millions of years ago. The early Indians gave it the name we know today. They called it "apasum," which means white animal.

Several opossum relatives still live in Mexico and Central and South America, but perhaps the most famous marsupials of all live in Australia. They are the kangaroo, wallaby, wombat, Tasmanian devil and the teddybear look-alike koala.

Opossum Country

Most North American opossums live in the warm southeastern parts of the United States. But in the last 100 years or so, opossums have started to move north into the New England states and southern Canada. Opossums can even be found as far west as California, Oregon, Washington and southern British Columbia.

Opossums often live on the edge of a forest or on farmlands. They do not stray far from a stream or marsh. Some opossums have even moved into suburbs, towns and cities, where they usually set up home in parks.

Opossums often climb up trees to escape from their enemies.

Sizing Up the Opossum

Imagine a white rat as big as a house cat. That is what the opossum looks like. A full-grown male opossum weighs as much as six kilograms (12 pounds), or about as much as a fat cat. From the tip of its nose to the end of its tail it measures 60 to 80 centimetres (24-32 inches). Female opossums are slightly smaller.

Bless My Whiskers

The opossum has four rows of cat-like whiskers—each about eight centimetres (3 inches) long—growing out from the sides of its nose and cheeks. And just like a cat's whiskers, the opossum's whiskers are sensitive feelers. This is especially important when the opossum is wandering through brush at night, in search of food. If it can get its head through a narrow opening without its whiskers touching, then the opossum knows it can probably squeeze the rest of its body through too.

Opossum Picnic

When it is hungry, the opossum keeps its round, pink nose close to the ground so that it can sniff out its dinner quickly. It will eat almost anything that flies, crawls, hops or even walks by.

Its favorite foods are insects, especially crickets, grasshoppers, beetles and butterflies. But it will also eat small animals such as earthworms, snails, salamanders, frogs and lizards. Even snakes are considered a tasty treat! An opossum on the prowl will raid birds' nests to feast on the eggs or young birds, and it will also hunt mice, moles, young rabbits and squirrels. In the city, the opossum often knocks over garbage cans and digs up vegetable gardens looking for food.

"Oh dear—a dead end."

The opossum also eats fruit and plants. It will gorge on berries and other fruit that have fallen to the ground, and if it is still hungry, it will climb trees in search of more. Opossums that live in the south particularly enjoy persimmons and pokeberries. And it is common to see them feeding on grasses, clover, seeds and nuts.

If there is lots of food available, an opossum's home range might only be as big as five hectares (12 acres). But during lean times it may wander over an area four times that big looking for food.

An apple's a treat that's hard to beat.

Fuzzy Fur

Most of the opossum's body is covered with a double-thick fur coat. The white outercoat of stiff, finger-length guard hair helps to keep the opossum dry. The inner coat of thick, short hair is warm and woolly. It traps in body heat. This inner coat can either be pure white or white tipped with black. The mixture of white and black fur gives the opossum its silvery gray color.

Like a cat, the opossum uses its rough tongue to groom its coat. First it licks its front paws clean and uses them to scrub its face. Then it usually sits on its haunches and gives its belly a good cleaning.

This untidy fellow is in need of a good grooming.

Double Grip

Imagine having your hands where your feet are and feet where your hands are. That may sound backwards to you, but the opossum finds it very useful.

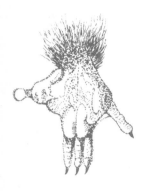

Rear paw

The opossum has a thumb on each of its back paws which means it can grip things the way you can with your hands. Having a thumb is a terrific help to a tree climber whose safety depends on hanging on. The opossum also has an extra "hand." Its tail can wrap around a branch while the opossum is high up in a tree, leaving its hands free to grab the next branch.

Getting up and down trees is no problem either. The opossum has long sharp claws on all of its fingers and toes, except its thumbs. It digs these claws into the tree bark for a good safe grip.

Hanging Around

The opossum is the only animal in North America that can hang upside down by its tail. Why it does this is not known. But it is easy to see how it does it. It simply wraps its tail around a tree branch and lets go with its hands.

If you see an opossum hanging upside down by its tail, you can be sure it is a young opossum. Full-grown opossums are too fat and heavy to hang from their tails. If they tried it—BONK—they would probably land head first on the ground.

"Look mom . . . no hands . . . or feet!"

Opossum on the Run

If you ran a race against an opossum, who would win? Probably you would. The fastest time ever recorded for an opossum was only 13 kilometres (8 miles) an hour.

But even if you could outrun an opossum, you probably would not be able to catch it. The opossum is built so low to the ground that it can easily duck under bushes and shrubs, squeeze into small holes in the ground, scurry into hollow logs, hide behind piles of rocks or even nip up a tree to avoid you.

A walking opossum is a real slowpoke. It has a plodding gait that looks awkward because it moves the two legs on the same side at the same time.

There are lots of good hiding places in this dense cover.

Opossum Hideaway

Opossums do not spend a lot of time and energy digging a den or building a home for themselves. Instead, they take over a burrow abandoned by a groundhog or skunk or move into a hollow log or even the hollow of a tree. In the city, an opossum might make its home under a house porch, in a garage or even inside a storm sewer.

Once it has moved in, the opossum lines its den with plenty of leaves and twigs for comfort and warmth. How does the opossum carry this bedding home? First, it gathers leaves in its front feet and pushes them under its body. Then it wraps its long, flexible tail around the leaves, picks them up and hurries home, carrying the load of leaves with its tail.

When its den is finished the opossum snoozes away the days in it.

Bundle Up!

The opossum is not built to withstand frosty weather. The bottoms of its feet are bare and so are its long, thin ears. And, except for a few stiff bristles, its tail is naked too. This is not a problem for opossums that live in warm climates, but what about those that have moved into cold-weather country?

If the weather gets really cold, an opossum spends up to two weeks at a stretch snuggled up in its den. It does not go out to search for food. Instead it lives off a thick layer of body fat that it built up by eating an extra lot in the fall. But in a long cold spell, the opossum must go out and look for food. Brrr! Many northern opossums have lost the tips of their ears and the end of their tails because of frostbite.

During winter an opossum may have to risk frostbite in order to get a drink.

"Playing Possum"

Owls, foxes and bobcats are just a few of the animals that consider opossums a tasty meal. To avoid these enemies, an opossum will often run for a safe hiding spot or up a tree. But as we have seen, opossums are not fast runners. So, to fool their pursuers, the opossum has come up with another trick. It flops over and plays dead. Since none of its enemies will eat a dead animal, the opossum often saves itself.

If you are ever lucky enough to see an opossum play dead, or "play possum," as it is sometimes called, here is what you would see. When the enemy gets too close, the opossum topples over on its side, lets its mouth drop open and often closes its eyes. It even slows down its breathing and its heartrate. The opossum acts so lifeless that it will not budge or even flicker its eyes if its enemy pokes it or picks it up in its mouth and shakes it.

However, sometimes the opossum gets mixed up. If the predator puts it back on the ground on the wrong side, it will forget it is supposed to be dead and flip over onto the other side. So much for playing dead!

This Opossum Means Business

If an opossum is cornered by an enemy and does not have a chance to "play possum," it may try to frighten off the attacker. It faces its enemy, opens its mouth wide to show off its sharp teeth and hisses and growls loudly.

The opossum even makes itself look bigger than it really is by standing up as tall as possible and holding its tail straight up. The sight of such a fierce-looking opossum is often enough to make most of its enemies think twice.

"Come any closer and you'll be sorry!"

Mating Time

The opossum is a loner and usually chooses to live by itself. The only time that adult opossums can be seen together is during mating season. When an opossum mates depends on where it lives. Opossums that live in the south mate from January to August. More northerly opossums mate between February and August.

Opossums usually mate only once during the mating season. But sometimes a female opossum may mate twice and have two litters in one season—the first in late February and the second in late July.

A Cozy Nursery

Just 13 days after mating, the female opossum is ready to give birth. She lines her den with plenty of leaves and twigs to make a cozy nursery. There she gives birth to as many as 20 babies at one time. She raises her babies alone, without any help from the male.

You could easily hold an entire litter of 20 opossums in a tablespoon! The newborn opossum measures just 14 millimetres (half an inch) long from one end to the other. That is about the same size as a honeybee.

The newborn opossum is rosy pink and hairless. Its ears and eyes are still closed and its back legs and tail are small stubs. But its front legs are well developed and come equipped with claws.

Everyone into the Pouch, Please

The first few moments of a baby opossum's life are quite busy. As soon as it is born, the mother opossum licks it very carefully. Next she licks her own stomach fur to make it moist and slippery. The baby, using the tiny claws on its front feet as mini-hooks, wriggles and squirms its way along this slippery path until it finds the fur-lined pouch on its mother's stomach. Then it crawls in.

With so many young it's quite a tight squeeze.

Home Sweet Pouch

The mother opossum's stomach pouch is like a big, warm, woolly pocket. She can open her pocket whenever she likes by simply relaxing her muscles and close it again by tightening them.

Hidden inside this pouch are 13 nipples arranged in the shape of a horseshoe. There are 12 nipples along the edge and one nipple in the centre.

Even though the opossum mother sometimes gives birth to as many as 20 babies at once, she can only feed 13. There is one nipple for one baby. Those that do not find a nipple do not survive.

Each newborn struggles to latch onto one of the mother's nipples.

Growing Up Inside a Pouch

Once inside its mother's pouch, the newborn opossum finds a nipple and immediately starts to drink its mother's rich milk. It will not let go of this nipple for about 60 days.

The baby grows very quickly, and life inside the pouch gets more and more crowded. About 14 days after birth, the baby starts to grow fuzzy, silvery fur. Its back legs and tail grow longer and stronger, and it gains weight steadily. But, it is not until the baby opossum opens its eyes—between the ages of 58 and 72 days—that it becomes curious about the outside world. It is only then that it lets go of the nipple and finally pokes its head outside the pouch.

This young opossum may live up to seven years.

Hello There, World!

Once out of the pouch, the baby opossum is still weak and quite helpless. And although it starts to explore the world, it does not stray far from its mother. Because its legs are still rather wobbly, it often rides piggy-back style, clinging with its tiny, but strong, claws to its mother's back.

Traveling this way, the mother takes all her babies out on short trips from the nest. During these outings, she shows them how to find food and climb trees.

"I'll get the hang of this yet!"

Moving Out

The baby opossum nurses until it is about 100 days old. When it is hungry, it just climbs into its mother's pouch and latches onto a nipple. Sometimes, if the mother is lying on her side sunning herself, the baby opossum hangs backwards out of the pouch and suns itself too, without letting go of the nipple.

The baby opossum grows and learns quickly. By the time it is 100 days old, it is ready to leave its mother and find a den of its own. Usually it does not wander far from its mother's den. But although it lives nearby, the young opossum does not spend time with its mother or brothers and sisters. Now it prefers to be on its own. When it is about eight months old it will be ready to mate and start a family of its own.

Words to Know

Den   Animal home.

Groom   To clean.

Guard hair   Long coarse hairs that make up the outer layer of an opossum's coat.

Home range   The area where an opossum looks for food.

Marsh   An area where the ground is soaked with water.

Marsupials   A family of animals whose females carry the young in a pouch until they are fully developed.

Mate   To come together to produce young.

Mating season   The time of year during which animals mate.

Muscles   Parts of the animal's body that help it move.

Nipple   The part of the mother's body through which a baby drinks her milk.

Pouch   The fur-lined pocket on the female marsupial where the babies live until they are developed.

Predator   An animal that lives by hunting other animals.

INDEX

Cover Photo: Steve Maslowski

Photo Credits: Karl H. Maslowski, pages 4, 7, 36, 39, 40; Steve Maslowski, pages 16, 19, 23, 27, 28, 43, 44; R.C. Simpson (Valan Photos), pages 8, 31, 35; Leonard Lee Rue IV (Miller Services), pages 11, 32; H.R. Hungerford, pages 12, 15, 21; Ontario Ministry of Natural Resources, page 24.

Printed and Bound in Italy by Lego SpA